A ROOKIE BIOGRAPHY

CHRISTOPHER COLUMBUS

A Great Explorer

By Carol Greene

CHILDRENS PRESS®

CHICAGO

This book is for Bryan Reat.

Painted about 1525, this picture is the closest likeness we have of Christopher Columbus.

LIBRARY OF CONGRESS
Library of Congress Cataloging-in-Publication Data

Greene, Carol.
    Christopher Columbus : a great explorer / by Carol Greene
      p. cm. — (A Rookie biography)
    Includes index.
    Summary: A biography of the fifteenth-century Italian seaman and
navigator who unknowingly discovered a new continent while looking for
a western route to India.
    ISBN 0-516-04204-1
    1. Columbus, Christopher—Juvenile literature. 2. Explorers—
America—Biography—Juvenile literature. 3. Explorers—Spain—
Biography Juvenile literature. 4. America—Discovery and exploration—
Spanish—Juvenile literature. [1. Columbus, Christopher. 2. Explorers.]
I. Dobson, Steve, ill. II. Title. III. Series: Greene, Carol. Rookie biography.
E111.G787   1989
970.01′5—dc19
[B][92]   88-37943
                                     CIP
                                     AC

Christopher Columbus
was a real person.
He was not the first
to discover America.
People already lived there.
But he was a great explorer.
This is his story.

TABLE OF CONTENTS

Genoa, Italy, was a busy port. Ships sailed
in and out of its harbor every day.

Christopher Columbus was born in this
room (above) in this house (right) in Genoa.

Chapter 1

Christopher Columbus Was Different

Ships sailed in
and ships sailed out
of the busy harbors
at Genoa, Italy.

Day after day,
a little boy watched them.
He had red hair,
blue eyes, and freckles.

This statue of Christopher Columbus as a young boy overlooks the city of Genoa.

His father was a weaver.
So were his grandfathers.
But Christopher Columbus
was different.
He wanted to go to sea.

When Columbus was young, mapmakers thought the world looked like this.

As soon as he could,
he worked on ships.
He learned about
sailing and maps.
And when he was 25,
he sailed off to Portugal.

There he married
a girl called Felipa.
He worked in a shop
making maps.
But he also made a plan.

Sailors told stories about sea monsters that attacked ships
when they sailed into unknown waters. Some people called the
waters to the south and west of Spain, the Sea of Darkness.

In the late 1400s,
people wanted to go
to the Indies.
That was their name
for India, China, and Japan.

The Indies had spices and gold.
There were strange sights,
such as people with feet
like umbrellas.
That's what people thought.

To get there, they said,
you must go around Africa.
Then you must sail east.

But Christopher Columbus
was different.
He wanted to sail west.

"I'll just sail across
the Ocean Sea," he thought.
(That's what people called
the Atlantic Ocean.)
"It won't take long.
Then I'll be at Japan."

Christopher Columbus

He didn't know how big
the Atlantic Ocean really was.
He didn't know about
North and South America
or the Pacific Ocean.

11

Columbus took his
plan to King John
of Portugal.
"Give me ships and
money," he said.
"And I will bring
you gold."

But the king said, "No."

So Columbus
went to Spain.
He took his plan
to Queen Isabella.

"Wait," said the queen.
She was busy
fighting a war.

Queen Isabella of Spain listened to Columbus.

Columbus waited
for six years.
At last she won the war.
Then she sent for him.

"All right,"
said the queen.
"You may have
your ships and money."

Chapter 2

A Happy Man

It didn't take Columbus
long to get ready.
He bought three ships:
the *Niña*, the *Pinta*,
and the *Santa Maria*.
He'd sail on the *Santa Maria*.

He hired men.
He put food, water,
and tools on the ships.
He also put on cats.
Ships always had rats.

A model of the *Santa Maria*

Many artists have drawn pictures of Columbus saying good-bye
to Queen Isabella and sailing off to discover a New World. How
are these pictures alike? How are they different?

The cabin Columbus lived in aboard the *Santa Maria*. At left is his sword. The flag of Spain is on his desk.

Then, on August 3, 1492,
Christopher Columbus
set sail.
He was a happy man.

The ships sailed for days.
The sailors saw a whale.
They saw lots of seaweed,
lots of birds,
and a shooting star.
Mostly they saw the sea.

Sometimes they got scared.
"Let's go back," they said.

About 1585 this artist drew this fantasy picture
showing Columbus calmly sailing through strange waters
surrounded by sea spirits and sea monsters.

But Columbus
smelled the air
and looked at the stars.
"Forward!" he said.
He was a happy man.

On September 25, someone yelled, "Land!" But it was only clouds.

On October 2, someone else saw land. He was wrong, too.

A sailor thinks
he sees land.

Columbus would not let his ships turn back.
He knew he would find land.

"Let's go back,"
said the sailors.
"No," said Columbus.

On October 11, Columbus thought
he saw a light.
But he wasn't sure.

Then, at 2 A.M. on October 12,
they *did* see land.
And that is when Columbus
was a *very* happy man.

Columbus and his crew land on San Salvador.

Chapter 3

Where Is Japan?

It was a little island.
Columbus knew that
it was not Japan.
He called it San Salvador.

Island people came
to see the ships.
Their feet did not
look like umbrellas.

But they wore no clothes.
They thought the sailors'
clothes were strange.

Drawing shows
Columbus trading
with the
island people.

They gave the sailors
thread, spears, and parrots.
The sailors gave them
beads, caps, and bells.

"Where is Japan?"
asked Columbus.
The island people didn't know.

Columbus and his crew explored the coast of Cuba.

So off sailed the ships.
They found more islands.
They saw strange things,
such as sea cows.

Today sea cows are
endangered animals.

At last they found
the big island of Cuba.
"It's not Japan,"
thought Columbus.
"But I think
it must be China."

He sent men out
to find the king—and gold.
All they found were huts
and more naked people.

Columbus in Cuba

So on sailed Columbus.
He found Hispaniola.
People there had some gold.
"This *must* be Japan,"
he thought.

Columbus in Hispaniola

The *Santa Maria* sank during a storm.

Then one night his ship,
the *Santa Maria*, sank.

"Build a fort,"
said Columbus.
"We'll leave 39 men here.
They can look for gold.
I'll go back to Spain
and get more ships."

The *Niña* and the *Pinta* sailed back to Spain.

So the *Niña* and the *Pinta*
sailed back to Spain.
It was a hard trip.
But they made it.

Columbus rode a horse
to the palace.
He brought parrots,
plants and shells,
six island people,
and a little bit of gold.

In 1493 Columbus showed his discoveries to
Queen Isabella and King Ferdinand.

"I have found
the Indies," he said.
And the king and queen
called him "Admiral of the Ocean."

Above: Columbus sails on his second trip to the New World.

The fort on Hispaniola was built from wood saved from the *Santa Maria*.

Chapter 4

Trouble

Columbus couldn't wait
to get back to his Indies.
He had 17 ships
and more than a
thousand men.
Think of the gold
they would find!

Instead, they found
a burned-down fort.
The 39 men were dead.

So Columbus went to
another part of Hispaniola.
"Find gold!" he told his men.
But they got sick—and mad.

In 1550 an artist drew this picture of the islands
Columbus had discovered in the New World.

Columbus looked for gold, too.
He didn't find much.
Maybe this *wasn't* Japan.
Maybe he should go
back to China.

He sailed to Cuba.
He found more islands.
But when he got back,
he found sick, angry men.
Then Columbus did
some cruel things.

He sent island
people to Spain
as slaves.
He made others
look for gold.
If they didn't
find enough,
he punished them.

**Indians flee in
fear of Columbus.**

At last, he went to Spain, too.
The king and queen
were not happy.
"Try again, Columbus,"
they said.

So he made a third trip.
He found the island
of Trinidad.
He found South America.
He thought he was close
to the Garden of Eden.

But his men in Hispaniola
still were not happy.
The king and queen sent
a man to see
what was wrong.
His name was Bobadilla.

Bobadilla arrested Columbus.
He put him in chains
and sent him back to Spain.

Chapter 5

The Last Trip

"Take off those chains,"
said the queen.
But she kept Columbus home
for almost two years.
Other men went exploring.
One even found India.

At last the queen
let Columbus go.
He had four ships now
and a new plan.

He would find a passage
through his Indies.
Then he'd sail ten days
and be in India.

At first, all went well.
Then a hurricane came.
Columbus made it through that.
But more storms came
and he *couldn't*
find the passage
to India.

Up and down the coast
of Central America
he sailed.
No passage.
So he looked for gold.

Columbus was driven out of Central America.

But the Central Americans
weren't too friendly.
Columbus and his men
had to leave.

The people of Jamaica were friendly.

They just made it to Jamaica.
Then their worn-out ships
fell apart.

They sat on Jamaica
for a year and five days.
At last a ship from Hispaniola
picked them up.
On November 7, 1504,
Columbus got back to Spain.

Queen Isabella
was born in
1451 and she
died in 1504.

But on November 26,
Queen Isabella died.
Columbus's exploring days
were over.

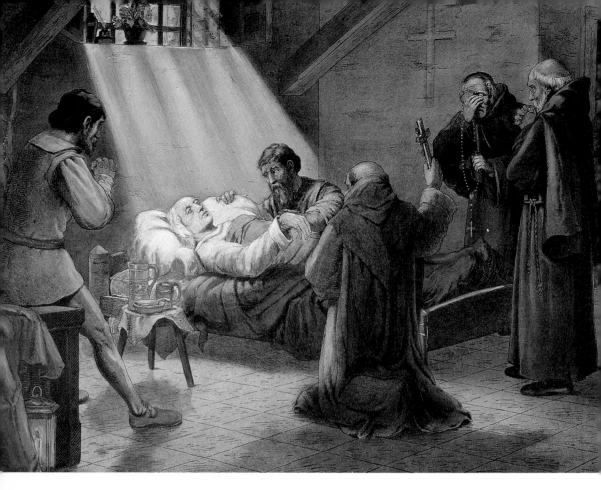

He'd made a lot of money.
But he wanted more.
"I found the Indies," he said.
"I found China.
I should get more reward."

He said that until
the day he died,
May 20, 1506.

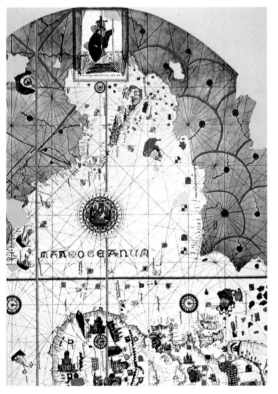

Below: Part of a map drawn in 1500 by Juan de la Cosa, a navigator on the *Niña* during its second voyage to the New World.

Christopher Columbus

He *didn't* find Japan.
He *didn't* find China.
He found
a whole New World.
But Christopher Columbus
never knew that.

45

Important Dates

1451 Born between August 25 and October 31
      in Genoa, Italy, to Domenico and
      Suzanna Columbus
1476 Went to Portugal
1478 Married Felipa Moñiz de Perestrello
1484 Went to Spain
1492 August 3—Sailed from Spain
      October 12—Found San Salvador
1493 Second trip
1498 Third trip
1500 Arrested and sent back to Spain
1502 Fourth trip
1503 Shipwrecked on Jamaica
1504 Rescued
1506 May 20—Died at Valladolid, Spain

INDEX

Page numbers in boldface type indicate illustrations.

PHOTO CREDITS

ABOUT THE AUTHOR

Carol Greene has degrees in English Literature and Musicology. She has worked in international exchange programs, as an editor, and as a teacher. She now lives in St. Louis, Missouri, and writes full time. She has published more than seventy books, most of them for children. Other Childrens Press biographies by Ms. Greene include *Louisa May Alcott, Marie Curie, Thomas Alva Edison, Hans Christian Andersen, Marco Polo,* and *Wolfgang Amadeus Mozart* in the People of Distinction series, *Sandra Day O'Connor, Mother Teresa, Indira Nehru Gandhi, Diana, Princess of Wales, Desmond Tutu,* and *Elie Wiesel* in the Picture-Story Biography series, and *Benjamin Franklin, Pocahontas,* and *Martin Luther King, Jr.* in the Rookie Biographies.